W9-DJN-743

Beta Phi Mu Chapbook Number Two

FINE BINDING IN AMERICA

by
Elbert A. Thompson
and
Lawrence S. Thompson

Published by Beta Phi Mu, 1956

the
story
of
the
CLUB
BINDERY

This is the second in a series of chapbooks published by Beta Phi Mu, National Library Science Honorary Fraternity, as a contribution to the art of book design and the literature of books and libraries.

Shortly after its founding in 1949, at the University of Illinois, the membership of Beta Phi Mu decided that in addition to its primary purpose of recognizing academic achievement in library science the society should also further the art of book design through a series of publications whose subject matter would be concerned with books and libraries.

The first volume in the chapbook series was CONTEMPORARY BOOK DESIGN, written and designed by Ralph Eckerstrom, and published in 1953. Mr. Eckerstrom, who is the art director of the University of Illinois Press, also designed this second volume.

E. A. Thompson is a bookbinder and plastics processor whose special interests include the history of American binding. He lives and works in Mineola, New York.

Lawrence S. Thompson, Director of the University of Kentucky Library, is a bibliologist whose interests range over almost the entire world of booklore, from fine bindings to skin bindings, from Kentuckiana to Scandinavica, from bibliokleptomania to bibliotaphy, ad infinitum.

Preface

This study of the Club Bindery represents the fruits of several years of research by the senior author. The junior author's contributions have been confined principally to matters of organization and style.

Of the many individuals who have given material assistance to this study the one surviving member of the Club Bindery, Thomas James Holmes of Burton, Ohio, deserves special recognition. Mrs. Robert Sterling (Ruth Hoe), Miss Marian Holden, and Mrs. Susan Hardy Plant have also contributed a great deal of information.

Full documentation and extensive quotations from original sources may be found in a longer version of this study which was issued on microcards as *The Club Bindery* (Rochester, University of Rochester Press, 1954; "ACRL Microcard Series," no. 14).

The University of Kentucky Research Fund has generously provided assistance in securing illustrations.

Elbert A. Thompson
Mineola, New York
Lawrence S. Thompson
Lexington, Kentucky

THE ART OF HAND BOOKBINDING came to North America almost simultaneously with the art of printing, and for almost two centuries both were cultivated in the same tradition of individual craftsmanship that prevailed in Europe as well as the new world. Early in the nineteenth century, however, the industrial revolution invaded the field of book production, and the rapid development of book manufacturing machinery after the Civil War compelled printers as well as binders to produce in quantity or go out of business. The few hand binders who inherited businesses from the earlier period soon learned that they could earn a far better living at edition binding than in the production of individual fine bindings.

1

By the 1870s and 1880s few hand bookbinders were in business anywhere in the country, and virtually all of them were trained in Europe. Moreover, the new immigrants soon learned that the most profitable business was not fine binding, but edition binding and library binding for the burgeoning publishing industry and public library movement. William Matthews, a Scot who was the leading hand binder from 1850 until the end of the century, earned his livelihood as superintendent of the bindery of D. Appleton and Company. Well trained young Britons such as James Macdonald and William Launder were encouraged by Matthews to come to this country, but they soon drifted into edition binding or a combination of hand and machine work. Cedric Chivers, Ernst Hertzberg, and Joseph Ruzicka, names now famous as library binders, received traditional training as hand binders in England, Germany, and Bohemia, but they quickly learned that their best opportunities lay in the new public library movement. A distinguished craftsman such as Otto Zahn never forsook his devotion to the practice and theory of fine binding, but he was to make his fortune as the president of a well known west Tennessee stationery firm. The attitudes of all of these men may be summarized in the comment of William Loring Andrews on Matthews: "The fine bindings he executed were mainly a relaxation, in which he indulged for the gratification of his cultured artistic taste and the accommodation of a few of his book-loving friends. So far as my knowledge extends, he never professed to make a *business* of special and elaborately tooled book-binding." (*Bibliopegy in the United States*, 1902)

It is something of a parodox that the industrialization of the United States forced the hand binder into edition and library binding but at the same time created a new class of bibliophiles who brought the golden age of book collecting to the western hemisphere. Of the great personalities of this period, J. P. Morgan, Henry Clay Folger, and Henry E. Huntington need no introduction, for they have left their books to world-famous libraries named for themselves. Perhaps the greatest of the entire group was Robert Hoe III, scion of the well-known family of printing machine manufacturers. Hoe was a collector by instinct and by choice from early youth, a familiar figure in the auction galleries of New York, Paris, and London, and a central personality in nearly all bibliophilic activities in New York from the eighties until his death in 1909. The now almost legendary Hoe Sale in 1911-12 fetched $1,932,056.60, a record never equalled in America and surpassed only by the sale of the celebrated Britwell Court Library in London (1910-27). The Hoe Collection was especially distinguished for early printed books and books representing the progress of the graphic arts, but there were also many other choice pieces ranging from emblem books to Filson's *Kentucky* (with the map).

Of the lesser bibliophiles of the age of Hoe, special mention should be made of Edwin Babcock Holden, the original guiding spirit of the Club Bindery. Had not Holden passed away at the early age of forty-four in 1906, he might well have become a collector whose shelves would

3

have rivalled Hoe's. A coal dealer by trade, Holden was also deeply interested in American portraiture and the iconography of Manhattan, and his collection in these fields was representative. Better known as a collector was Beverly Chew (1850-1924), an official of the Metropolitan Trust Company of New York and other financial institutions and master of a library of choice first editions of American and English literature. His influence was enormous, and his judgment was respected by bibliophiles and booksellers on both sides of the Atlantic. Marshall C. Lefferts (1848-1928) also brought together an unusual collection of older English literature and early Americana. Winston H. Hagen (1859-1918) was primarily concerned with collecting the great monuments of English literature from Chaucer to the present day, but he also included many another rare volume for its sheer beauty. As Beverly Chew explained in his foreword to the sale catalogue (May, 1918), Hagen was almost the prototype of the book lover. Frederic Robert Halsey (1847-1918) specialized in English, American, and French literature; and the 20,000 volume Halsey collection is one of the capstones of the library of Henry E. Huntington, who acquired it in 1915. Of the many other great names from the golden age of American book collecting only a few more may be mentioned here on account of their association in some way with the Club Bindery: Walter Gilliss, the noted New York printer; General Rush C. Hawkins, founder of the Annmary Brown Memorial in Providence; Samuel Putnam Avery, founder of Columbia's Avery Architectural Library and a special connoisseur of fine binding; Theodore Hoe Mead, manufacturer, author, and collector; Junius S. Morgan, the one member of the Morgan group who showed a special interest in the Club Bindery; Arthur Hawley Scribner, an executive of Charles Scribner and Sons; Henry William Poor, at whose sale in 1908-09 many fine bindings were made available to American collectors, and S. W. Marvin, one of the founders of the Grolier Club.

Men such as these could afford to buy magnificent books which deserved the same care that a Grolier or a De Thou required for their collections. Their great wealth enabled them to buy fine books at a pace which could not be matched by the productivity of the few hand binders in the United States, and they were compelled to send their treasures to London or Paris for superior quality of binding and restoration. The risk of loss or damage in transportation and the waste of time was irksome. Moreover, correspondence could never take the place of personal discussion between collectors and binders. In view of these circumstances, a group of bibliophiles, recruited mainly from those who had been active in the Grolier Club since its founding in 1884, decided that the only answer to their problems lay in the establishment of a superior hand bindery with craftsmen devoting full time to their work.

After long discussions of the problem, a group centering around Edwin B. Holden decided that it would be feasible to set up a bindery in New York that could turn out work comparable to anything done in Europe. It was to be given the simple name of the Club Bindery, although there was no official connection with the Grolier Club. The task of creating a formal organization began in 1895. Holden sent out a printed prospectus with letters to members of the Grolier Club. The organizers hoped to distribute the stock as widely as possible to enable many individuals to take advantage of the facilities offered by the Club Bindery, since the right to use the bindery was limited to stockholders. Ideally, they would have liked to have seen one share in the hands of each of some two hundred individuals, but this could hardly be expected in view of the limited membership of the Grolier Club (about three hundred at that time). The appeal for participation in the Club Bindery met with encouraging success. As early as July, 1895, it was possible to place an order for supplies, including such items as leathers, French gold, and marbled papers, with Louis De Jonge and Company of New York.

In August French materials were ordered. James O. Wright, one of the stockholders, was in Paris and was able to make arrangements with the well-known binding supply house of Terquem to act as agents for the Club Bindery. Wright advised Terquem that only materials of the highest quality would be acceptable, and this rule was followed strictly throughout the business life of the Club Bindery. In October, 1896, for example, Holden registered a firm complaint with Terquem for sending split leather and insisted that in the future all skins be sent in the full thickness.

The relatively abundant capital back of the company enabled it to carry an ample stock of the best materials. Since the directors and stockholders were men whose business interests frequently took them to Europe, they could take advantage of exceptional opportunities in France and England to secure all sorts of superior materials. At the same time they soon learned from experience that it was necessary in Paris to select materials personally, without regard for prices, since the dealers held back the best for French craftsmen.

Corporation papers were filed on 8 August 1895 by Edwin B. Holden, Walter Gilliss, Robert Hoe, and Richard H. Lawrence. The authorized capital was $10,000, consisting of two hundred shares valued at $50 each. The actual amount of capital with which the Club Bindery began business was one hundred shares, or $5,000. The directors for the first year were Edwin B. Holden, Walter Gilliss, and Junius S. Morgan, all of New York, and they also served as president, secretary, and treasurer respectively. They received no salaries. At a later meeting of the stockholders the number of directors was increased to five with the election of Beverly Chew and Marshall C. Lefferts to this office.

Although it was not possible to issue two hundred shares to two hundred individuals, every precaution was taken to insure that no one individual should hold more than five shares and that the stock should be owned only by men who were genuinely interested in fine bookbinding. That the latter objective was achieved is obvious from the following list of stockholders: Samuel P. Avery, five shares; William L. Andrews, four shares; Fred A. Castle, one share; Beverly Chew, one share; Thomas G. Evans, one share; Walter Gilliss, five shares; Richard M. Hoe, five shares; Marshall C. Lefferts, five shares; S. W. Marvin, one share; Theodore H. Mead, two shares; Arthur H. Scribner, two shares; James O. Wright, two shares; and Junius S. Morgan, one share. All of these men were prominent collectors and aggressively interested in furthering the work of the new organization. Holden bore the principal burden of getting production started, and as the first president of the Club Bindery he managed its affairs incidentally to his own business.

In addition to the stated objective of obtaining work which could rival anything produced abroad, the founders of the Club Bindery also hoped to introduce a new note in binding design in the United States and to realize their purposes as economically and as expeditiously as was consistent with good craftsmanship. Holden hoped and intended that orders for simpler bindings would supplement those for fine work, for he wished to build up a broad clientele among collectors whose resources were somewhat more modest than those of a Hoe or a Morgan. He doubted the wisdom of permitting the bindery to be dependent upon the business of a few wealthy patrons, and subsequent events proved the legitimacy of this viewpoint. The Club Bindery might have had a longer history if Holden's advice had been followed consistently.

It was quite natural that the officers should go to their fellow Grolier Club member, William Matthews, for advice on setting up the shop and securing craftsmen. Matthews gave generously of his time and knowledge, and at his suggestion Frank Mansell, finisher, and R. W. Smith, forwarder, were employed. The bindery was located at 31 Broad Street, a site which was probably chosen to suit the convenience of the directors, most of whom had offices in lower Manhattan. Although the quarters may have seemed rather cramped, they were spacious by comparison with those of many contemporary French binders, not a few of whom worked in a single room in their private homes.

Mansell, one of the best designers and finishers in the United States in his day, was born in Oxford, England, in 1861 and was educated in the City of London School. He was apprenticed to his father, W. Mansell, a well known London binder. In 1883 the junior Mansell and his wife, May, came to the United States to accompany a brother who made the voyage on the advice of a physician. They decided to remain in this country, and Frank Mansell, like Alfred and William Launder, James Macdonald, and other young English immigrant binders, found employment with William Matthews at Appleton's. A little more than a decade later Matthews thought enough of his protégé to recommend him to Holden. Of R. W. Smith we know almost nothing other than that he took a prominent part in some binding exhibitions held in the nineties.

Mansell and Smith began their work with the best equipment and supplies that their wealthy patrons could give them. Although they were not destined to continue their employment into the days of the height of the Club Bindery's fame and prestige, we do have abundant evidence of the high quality of their work in Henri Pène du Bois' *American Bookbindings in the Library of Henry W. Poor.* In this handsome book printed by Frank E. Hopkins at the Marion Press in 1903 there are illustrations of their work printed in full color and overstamped with gold leaf to reproduce the original gold tooling in every detail.

Although Robert Hoe held no more stock than several other men, his enthusiasm about the possibilities of the project waxed rapidly. In an essay in the first volume of *The Bibliographer* (1902), "Of Bibliophilism and the Preservation of Books," written under the pseudonym of Henry French, the great collector expressed quite clearly his ideas about the binding of fine books and indicated what he and his contemporaries expected of the Club Bindery:

After all that can be said in favor of retaining books in their original covers, there are very many which for their preservation demand rebinding, even as old rags should give place to proper clothing. . . . Every collector . . . if he takes a just view of the matter, cannot do otherwise than consider himself as their temporary custodian, and wish to transmit them to his successors if possible in better condition than when he acquired them. . . . Perhaps some critics may still cavil at what they consider a too lavish expenditure, and still vaunt the superiority of the "original cover." If these are good, any renewal of them is unnecessary, but as all books must have bindings, it is surely better to have them well done and even elaborately decorated, no matter when their covers may be placed upon them. The better they are, the better the chance of the survival of the volumes, and the best will wear out soon enough.

Several months after work began at the Club Bindery, the stockholders held a meeting at which examples of the bindery's work were displayed and discussed. It was concluded that the books on display were equal or superior to anything that was being done in the United States, but still not on a par with the best European work. Some excellent finishing was being done, but the forwarding or the actual building of the book did not measure up to the standards set by the leading bibliophiles of the day. General Rush C. Hawkins was so disappointed that he instructed Holden to cancel his subscription to one share in capital stock. Holden patiently explained to the General that one could hardly expect the best possible work after only six months of operation, for he felt that the new organization should grow naturally and earn its way.

11

Robert Hoe, more impatient, wanted immediate perfection, and Holden agreed that Hoe might take more responsibility for the operation of the Club Bindery in view of the latter's energy and enthusiasm for the project. Since Hoe travelled extensively and was well acquainted with the work of many European binders, he was in a position to look for craftsmen who could meet the standards set for the new bindery. His search led him to Henri Hardy, an employee of the noted firm of E. Mercier in Paris, and in April, 1896, Hardy and his wife sailed for New York. In selecting Hardy, Hoe expected to use him as a nucleus around whom a highly skilled staff might be built.

Henri Hardy was born in Paris in 1854, and at an early age he was placed in a monastery at Château de Creuilly, Calvados, Normandy, to study for the priesthood. The prospects of a clerical career did not appeal to him, and he ran away and returned to Paris, where he was apprenticed as a bookbinder in his father's shop from 1869 to 1876. During two years of this period he attended a course of lectures at the École des Beaux Arts, studying design and following the general curriculum. From 1876 to 1878 he worked with Charles Meunier; from June, 1878, to March, 1882, with T. Smeers; from 1882 to 1891, with Michel Ritter; from 1891 to 1892, with Dupré; and from 1893 to 1896, with E. Mercier.

Hardy worked under Mansell for a short time after his arrival, but he soon proved to be such an able craftsman that he was made foreman of the bindery. In addition to his ability as a binder, he was a colorful personality and a man of strong character. From early childhood he had read avidly the great works on French literature and history. Thomas J. Holmes, who did not join the staff until 1902, has vivid recollections of Hardy's discourses on literature at lunch. Rabelais and some of Balzac appealed to his sense of humor; Walter Scott (in French translation) and Dumas to his love of the colorful past; Montaigne to his high standards of personal morality; Voltaire to his realism. The characteristically Gallic qualities of Villon and La Fontaine endeared them to Hardy as his favorite poets, and the writings of Anatole France and Ernest Renan broadened his personal outlook on life. The significance of Hardy's wide reading and understanding of literature is reflected in many of his designs.

Hardy's national background, his background in French literature, his sense of the artistic, and his remarkable ability in his chosen craft appealed to Hoe as qualities suited to his own temperament. Hoe was as deeply interested in the literary content of his books as he was in their typography, their rarity, and their external dress or condition. His books were valuable as physical specimens, but at the same time they were read and understood by their owner. As a printing machine manufacturer, Hoe had brought his library together to illustrate the progress of the graphic arts;

but at the same time his collection included many a noble monument of literature and learning acquired for its own sake.

Although Hoe figured more and more prominently in the activities of the Club Bindery, Holden still administered its affairs. He was a cautious executive, and this quality served well to offset possible dangers in Hoe's enthusiasm. In July, 1897, Hoe wanted to employ the noted Parisian binder Cuzin, but Holden pointed out that it would be impossible to bring him to the United States on such definite terms of agreement as Hoe proposed without violating the contract labor law.

Nevertheless, the search for outstanding craftsmen went forward, and in 1897 Hoe, on Hardy's recommendation, ob-

tained the services of Léon Maillard, considered by some to have been the best finisher in Paris in his day. Maillard came from a family of binders, and after learning the rudiments of the craft in his father's shop, he worked under Cuzin, Gruel, and Marius Michel. Although he was not of an original turn of mind, it is doubtful whether there has ever been a finisher who could reproduce any given design in such perfection as Maillard could. He was particularly partial to Grolieresque bindings.

It was not always easy for Holden to control the temperamental Frenchmen who had little concept of the orderly management of business affairs. On one occasion Maillard assumed too much authority in ordering materials directly from Terquem, and Holden reprimanded him sharply. On several occasions Maillard threatened suicide, and ultimately he actually did destroy himself. The superior qualities of the Frenchmen, however, were highly appreciated, and other binders suffered by comparison with them. In February, 1898, Holden wrote to B. F. Stevens of London concerning one Taylor, an applicant for work as a forwarder with the Club Bindery, pointing out that a sample of Taylor's work was considerably below the standard set for the Club Bindery. In April, 1897, the Grolier Club had held an exhibition of American bookbinding, and the exhibitors included Blackwell, Bradstreet, William Matthews, R. W. Smith, Alfred Matthews, Otto Zahn, Henry Stikeman, Evelyn Hunter Nordhoff, and the Club Bindery. The Club Bindery's sponsors felt that there had been a very marked improvement in the forwarding department under Hardy's foremanship, and they were satisfied that Hardy and his assistants were turning out the finest binding in the western hemisphere.

Still the directors of the Club Bindery were not quite satisfied with the workmanship of the group as a whole. They felt, quite properly, that improvement should have come more rapidly than it did. There had been no indication of any truly creative designing. Maillard's interpretation and execution of the designs given to him could not be excelled, but he himself lacked originality. Mansell, still working as a finisher, was an able craftsman, but he followed the conventional patterns of book decoration that had been handed down for centuries, staying especially close to the English traditions which had always been predominant in American binding. There were other quite capable binders in New York who, given the time, could do comparable work in the same tradition; and elsewhere in the country there were men such as Hertzberg, Ruzicka, and Zahn who could do equally fine work in the German manner. Therefore, the directors felt that they should secure the services of craftsmen with greater skill if they were to continue to surpass local productions and ultimately to equal those of the continental binders. Hoe leaned definitely toward French binders, and at a meeting at which these problems were discussed it was decided to look again to the continent for new talent.

Since Mansell was doing more or less routine finishing, the directors did not feel that he should receive a salary equal to that of Maillard, who had become head finisher. In August, 1898, his wages were reduced, and he left shortly thereafter to accept a position in Boston where he worked until his death. Soon after Mansell's resignation the Club Bindery secured a replacement in Adolf Dehertog, a Parisian binder who had received his early training in Brussels and who was employed on the recommendation of Maillard and Hardy.

In the course of the next two years the productions of the Club Bindery not only met the unusually high standards of the directors but also attained a degree of excellence never surpassed in the western hemisphere. Under the constant critical supervision of the directors and patrons a large number of soul-satisfying bindings, unusual in design and execution, were produced. In 1900 Dodd, Mead and Company held an exhibition of about seventy books completed at the Club Bindery, and the general consensus was that nothing better was being done in Europe. The *New York Times* "Saturday Review of Books and Art" for 21 April 1900 was unusually complimentary of the books exhibited here and singled out three bindings for special praise.

As a result of the Dodd, Mead exhibition of 1900, the quantity of work brought to the Club Bindery increased substantially. The organization grew and added personnel, and problems of expanding working space, taxes, and other annoyances that are ever with business men plagued Holden. In 1897 the bindery moved from Broad Street to 13 West Twenty-Eighth Street and in 1901 it moved again to 114 West Thirty-Second Street, not far from Hoe's residence at 11 East Thirty-Sixth Street.

By the turn of the century the staff had grown to ten. In addition to Hardy, Dehertog, and Léon Maillard, there were Paul Maillard, a finisher whose skill was barely short of that of his brother, Léon; Charles Micolci, a coverer and assistant finisher from Switzerland, with experience in Paris, but lately in charge of the government bindery in Port-au-Prince, Haiti; Anna Berger, who did the mending, repairing, and washing of the leaves; Mary Neill, book sewer; Cornelia A. Hopkins, bookkeeper and manager, the only working member of the Club Bindery with any sense for business; Gebhard Raith, a lad who had come to the bindery about a year after it was established and applied himself well enough to be a second assistant finisher after Micolci; and one Verley, a Belgian who did routine work at the bindery until he resigned early in 1903.

Anna Berger received her training at the Club Bindery under the tutelage of Henri Hardy himself. She could take a mildewed, foxed, time-stained volume, wash out the stains, re-size and re-tint the leaves, and restore them to their original crispness, cleanness, and strength. Her entire time was given to this process of restoration. She filled worm holes skillfully, mended broken and torn leaves, and by careful matching of paper from old fragments could restore missing portions until the leaves appeared whole and new, with scarcely a trace of the mending.

Mary Neill took the books apart as they came in for rebinding. She mended broken folds and old sewing holes with narrow strips of very thin Japan paper pasted skillfully along the folds of the leaves. Every book that the Club Bindery bound during the years of her employment received this careful restoration of the damaged folds by Mary Neill. The most important part of her work was sewing, a job for which she was probably trained in New York before coming to the Club Bindery. However, her consummate skill at sewing on raised bands—all the full bindings done at the Club Bindery were sewn in this manner—was acquired from instruction by Henri Hardy, assisted probably by Madame Hardy, who worked in the bindery for a short while between April and October, 1896, when her daughter Susan was born. Still another task of Mary Neill was to work the head-bands of vari-colored silk.

As second assistant finisher, Gebhard Raith took the book from the finisher after all the tooling was completed. He pasted on end papers, inserted the silk linings, if any, and made boxes or slip cases when required.

Cornelia Hopkins kept a record of every binding, noting materials, number of hours spent on it as recorded on time sheets, for whom the job was done, and the final charges for it. She also kept a record of the hours of the employees and their rates. Since her death in the 1940s no one seems to know what has happened to the records of the Club Bindery.

By 1902 the reputation of the bindery had spread to bibliophilic circles in all quarters of the western world. T. J. Cobden-Sanderson had heard about the work of the Club Bindery. When he visited the United States, he made it a point to call on Robert Hoe, who escorted him through the shop. Cobden-Sanderson expressed both surprise and amazement that such work could be done in the United States. It is true that the craftsmen were neither Americans nor trained in America; but, nevertheless, the work was being done here.

That the fame of the Club Bindery was spreading rapidly may also be seen in the correspondence between Walter Gilliss, official secretary of the organization during its entire existence, and a young Englishman named Thomas James Holmes who was ambitious to try his luck in America. Holmes wrote to inquire about a position, and he received the customary reply that he would have to come without a contract. This he did, and he landed in New York on 12 October 1902. He immediately went to work as a forwarder and an edge gilder. When he met Hoe, the latter said, "We want good work, but we give you time." Hoe's favoritism for French binders involved no narrow prejudice, for he was willing to employ a good man, regardless of his origins.

Holmes was born in Newcastle on 26 December 1874. His first few months of apprenticeship as a binder were spent with David Dilworth of Newcastle and subsequently with George Thomas Bagguley, Dilworth's successor, from 1887 to 1895. Bagguley is well known for having developed a process of tooling vellum in color, particularly suitable for the treatment of vellum doublures. He named the process the "Sutherland Binding" for one of his patronesses, Millicent, Duchess of Sutherland. Upon leaving Newcastle young Holmes joined the staff of Rivière in London and served there from 1895 to 1899. He was again with Bagguley from 1899 to 1902, and during this period he won a diploma and a bronze medal for a binding exhibited at the Paris International Exposition in 1900. For a few months in 1902 he worked for Joseph Zaehnsdorf in London.

Prior to Holmes' arrival at the Club Bindery all books were sent out for edge gilding, and it is obvious from Club Bindery books of the period 1895-1902 which we have examined that the gilding was not too carefully done. Whether it was due to excessive haste or to deficient skill on the part of New York edge gilders cannot be definitely ascertained. One suspects both faults. After 1902 every operation of the Club Bindery was performed in the shop by members of the staff. Each book was complete in every way, and the whole binding process was carried on without outside help or advice. It is to the eternal credit of the new forwarder, or "l'Anglais" as the Frenchman called him, that he was never lured by the glitter of the finisher's art and only did those jobs at which he considered himself competent. Even in his apprentice days he never sought to practice the intricacies of the art of color tooling on vellum. Holmes has described his views in a private communication:

I sought to learn how the back of the book was formed and shaped so as to maintain its arch intact for durability, and still permit the book to be opened and read. I confess that I was a born reader and naturally looked on the book as a vehicle for conveying the thoughts of the author to the reader. The feeling was forced upon me that a book badly printed on poor ugly paper was an insult to author and reader alike. But if the book were of fine paper restful to the eye, printed with well-designed, beautiful type, large enough to be read easily, and bound in durable covers decorated

19

with modest taste, then the beauty of the book lends added charm to the author's eloquence and power. My friend Henri Hardy scorned this low utilitarian doctrine, and right eloquently did he set forth the claim that a fine binding is an object of art in itself, to be treated and treasured as such. "It is for preservation but not for reading," said he. I respected his view, and many collectors would endorse it, Mr. Robert Hoe foremost among them. While aiming to attain perfection in my forwarding at the Club Bindery, I followed Mr. Hardy's concepts and instructions, of course, and not my own ideas of construction where these varied. The traditions followed were still French. My low-down plebian utilitarian views led me on to other fields.

These "low-down plebian utilitarian views" led our forwarder in later years to a comprehensive study of the history of book preservation up to the development of the printed book. In October, 1946, he delivered a memorable lecture on the subject before the Honorary Consultants of the Army Medical Library (Armed Forces Medical Library) and later repeated it for the Rowfant Club. The lecture is printed in the *Proceedings* of the Honorary Consultants.

After Verley's departure early in 1903 Holmes was the sole forwarder in the Club Bindery until its end in 1909. In the course of his work he became especially interested in the problems of collation, the study of the correct sequence of the printed sheets as they come from the printer to form the book. This interest led him to bibliography, the queen of the book sciences. In 1941 his achievements were recognized by Trinity College in Hartford, Connecticut, which awarded him the honorary degree of doctor of letters for his bibliographical work on the Mathers.

Reference has been made to a difference between American binding methods, patterned on English traditions, and the French tradition. A brief definition of some of the points of distinction will be helpful in understanding the work of the Club Bindery. In

English bindings the boards are made as flat as possible, a situation which is, of course, the ideal one. However, when these flat boards are subjected to all the variations of heat and moisture created for modern homes and libraries, they tend to warp or curl slightly outwards at the edges away from the leaves. In turn, the leaves themselves begin to curl up and become dog-eared at the corners. With the appearance of these elements of untidiness the book invites neglect and disrespect, and it soon becomes scuffed and dirty, well on its way to the pulper.

The boards in a typical French binding contain an additional lining on their inner sides, and this lining draws and curves the edges of the boards inward towards the body of the book. This inward curvature resists any tendency to bend outwardly, and at the same time grasps the body of the book firmly to pre-

21

vent damage to the leaves. At times this inward curving can be overdone so that the boards clutch the fore-edges of the book like a pair of shells, while the center of the boards is humped up, thus leaving the book loose at the top and bottom, inviting dust, moisture, and insects.

The French thought of binding as a permanent protection for a book and developed an extremely round back. It held the book firmly in shape and prevented wear upon the sewing. To prepare a smooth ground for fine tooling and also to discourage opening the book too readily (a movement which could mar the tooling), the round back was lined in the panels between the raised bands with layers of cheese cloth and paper, sometimes even with vellum. This lining was then sandpapered to an extreme smoothness in preparation for the cover leather. In modern times this practice was emphasized by Trautz-Bauzonnet and was followed by most French binders through the first decade of this century. It is true that this form of high, round, and tight back rendered the book difficult to open and almost impossible to read, but the binding stood as a showpiece, and the book was preserved.

In the English traditions no definite tendency for a high, round, and tight back ever asserted itself. The greatest of the modern English binders, T. J. Cobden-Sanderson, even went so far as to advocate a flat back. Probably the first modern English binder to recognize the importance of a firm back was Rivière, who put into his bindings what he called a "thick, firm shoulder." This construction avoided the high, round French back and still produced a firm shoulder which held the back in shape and permitted the book to be opened readily for reading. To facilitate easier opening, sewing on raised bands had long been discontinued in England. Sunken bands with open-back linings were practically universal in England and America except in the rarest instances.

There were numerous other points of difference between the French and the Anglo-American traditions of hand bookbinding, some of which will be noted further on in this essay, while others are too detailed to describe here. In all respects, however, the French traditions tended generally to demand more thorough work and elaborate treatment, while the Anglo-American methods gave in at all points to time and labor-saving short-cuts. By the same token, the Anglo-American product, in general, was of lower quality than the French. Always, however, we must reckon with varying degrees of skill on the part of individual craftsmen, whatever their national background.

The leather used by the Club Bindery for covers was from carefully selected skins, prepared, dyed, and finished slowly and patiently by hand. The other materials, the finest quality of sewing thread, board, paper, and gold leaf, came from the best supply houses in France. With the finest materials at their disposal, the craftsmen in the Club Bindery were also meticulously careful in going through all the preliminary stages in the preparation of a book for an honest binding: cleaning or washing the pages (if an old book); filling worm holes; repairing and squaring the sheets; special sewing; forwarding or shaping the form of the book; and lacing in the boards. It is probably easier to deceive the amateur in these preliminary stages of a binding than in its decoration, where imperfections in tooling are immediately obvious. No thoroughly good bookbinding can be produced without a corresponding expenditure of time, effort, and money for good materials.

Although machine split leather makes for greater ease and speed in the covering process, the end result is apt to be shoddy. Thus Hardy always used the full original thickness of his leathers and would not tolerate split leather. What little paring of the leather that occurs in his bindings is at the edges for turning-in and at the points which were to fit over the spine of the book. Even this operation was performed in a way to make an almost right angle cut, with no shaving of the leather in the manner followed by most other American binders of the day. There was a very slight shaving from the center to the edges of the boards. Léon Maillard and the other finishers could do their best work with a cushion of leather that would allow deep tool impressions, sinking well into the surface of the skin.

Léon Maillard was widely acknowledged as the best finisher of his day. His tooling was solid, deep and lustrous as molten gold. He obtained this striking and inimitable effect by the repeated application of the warm engraving tools to the impressions of the pattern until he had actually burnished the refined gold filaments of the tool's design. Holmes has said that he never knew another finisher who could execute this exceptionally difficult feat. Certainly no finisher trained in the Anglo-American style of flat tooling in single impressions would even attempt to practice the method followed by Maillard. Holmes has provided a detailed account of Maillard's methods:

Léon Maillard's procedure was something in this order: First he would impress the tools upon a sheet of paper the size of the cover to be finished. Then he laid the tooled paper upon the cover and tipped the paper down at the corners with paste. The tools were then applied to their previous prints upon the paper and impressed sufficiently to leave their imprints in the cover leather. The paper was then removed and the tools reapplied to sharpen and deepen their impressions in the leather cover. The design at this point was already tooled in blind upon the cover. If the design, or parts of it, were intended to be left in blind, Léon Maillard would not be satisfied. He would moisten the leather with a damp sponge and retool the impressions to sharpen and deepen them still more. If the design was intended for gilding, then he would trace the lines with white of egg glair, using a camel hair pencil or fine brush. He would oil the leather very slightly with a pad of cotton, then lay on his gold leaf two layers at a time. A single layer would break along the lines of the tool impressions. He would lay on four or six layers of gold leaf until the tool impressions were completely lined in every tiny surface. The tools were heated to a little less than that of a laundering iron (Cobden-Sanderson said one should be able to touch the tool) and were then applied to the impressions. Léon Maillard would rock the tool gently and firmly until every part had been fully impressed and the gilt design thoroughly burnished. To facilitate this gentle and firm rocking or rolling motion, his tools were cut with a slightly spherical surface. This slightly spherical surface of finishing tools probably was in more or less common use in Paris, although it was unknown in England and in the United States at that time. By repeated impressions of his tools Léon Maillard obtained a brilliance that was unrivalled.

Léon Maillard would burnish the surface of his tools before use. A tool with a dull surface cannot leave a high burnished impression.

Although this great craftsman could imitate any of the classical designs used in the various styles of book cover decoration down through the centuries, usually far better than the original masters, he had no characteristic style of his own. The intensity with which he worked on the tooling of a design made him quite temperamental, and he insisted on working entirely alone. When the bindery moved to its Thirty-Second Street location, Maillard had his own room with two outside windows. The windows and the door were kept shut while he was at his bench.

Among the numerous artists employed to draw designs was the well known Louis J. Rhead. One of his outstanding designs was used on the Knickerbocker *History of New York* in two dark green levant morocco volumes bound for Holden and now in the possession of his daughter, Marian Holden. All of the original designs for cover and doublure and the tracings used for the tooling are preserved in the book. The tools were cut especially for this binding. The cover design, consisting of tulips and leaves in gold, forms a panel made from small tools. However, it is the doublure which attracts particular interest. In a field of light brown crushed levant, four white tulips with streaks of red are inlaid, one in each corner. They are surrounded by leaves in two shades of green. The Grolier Club seal in red, blue, and gold is inlaid on the front leather fly-leaf. Another unusual feature of the binding is that it carries the little used Club Bindery seal in gold on the back leather fly-leaf. In passing it might be noted that Holden himself was a designer of no mean ability. In addition to a number of title pages, he also designed the covers for some of his own bindings.

Since by 1902 the bindery was doing almost no work for anyone but Robert Hoe, many of the designs were drawn by a man who was employed in the drafting department of R. Hoe and Company. It was Hoe's opinion that the design should give the feeling of "oneness," that no one part should stand out over any other part. He was thoroughly conversant with the kinds and styles of bindings of all periods and could tell instantly whether a design was appropriate for a given book. His interest in these problems is brought out strongly in his lecture on "Bookbinding as a Fine Art," delivered before the Grolier Club on 26 February 1885.

One of the most frequent designers was none other than Henri Hardy. He could not handle the tools over the gold leaf as well as Léon or even Paul Maillard, but he was an artist and could draw anything from a simple sketch to an elaborate design. He was careful enough to keep several scrapbooks, one of which contains original sketches ranging from his days as an art student in Paris up through his retirement. Some of these original sketches can be recognized on books now in the Spencer Collection of the New York Public Library and elsewhere.

In the hand finishing of bindings it has been the tradition for the finisher to build up his design by the impression of small and simple tools. By the manipulation of lines, curves, leaves, and florets an endless variety of patterns may be evolved. Nevertheless, the old elements of pattern grow stale, and now and then something fresh and new is desired. It was for this reason that Hoe ordered original designs, not for small tools, but for a unified treatment of an entire side. Special tools were engraved for the execution of these designs. With a new design in hand Léon Maillard would mark off the portions from which the individual tools were to be cut. In a number of instances a whole set of tools was designed and made for a single book, and the set was never used again. Only the patrons of the Club bindery could have afforded such extravagance. In almost every case these tools were quite large, since Léon Maillard had a greater facility in using large tools than any other finisher. Great muscular strength was necessary to use them, but the finished effect was superior to what was obtainable from the use of many small tools. After the design had been so marked, it was sent to the best engravers in Paris and was cut exactly as indicated.

An outstanding example of Club Bindery work which nearly came to grief was Hoe's unique vellum copy of Hawthorne's *The Scarlet Letter*, now in the Spencer Collection. The illustrations consisted of fifteen color plates, fifteen original water colors by A. Robaudi and C. Graham, fifteen plate proofs in black, five plate proofs in different tones, and a small trial sketch by Robaudi. The binding of citron levant morocco has its sides enclosed within an ornate frame of fillets and flowers in rich mosaic design, with the flowers in dark blue, red, and white morocco. The doublure, also in citron levant, has a plain center panel within two fillets, and Hoe's monogram is at the bottom. The back is lettered and inlaid in colors in a corresponding design. Between the gilt lines at the bottom of the front doublure is the inscription, "Club Bindery, Léon Maillard, finisher, 1904." The book was assembled and forwarded by Holmes, covered by Hardy, and edges are gilt in the rough (an exceedingly difficult task). Hoe, following a Parisian fancy, favored rough gilt on all his modern books.

A near accident befell this beautiful volume in the forwarding. Holmes was attempting to build a rounded back and had to remove some of the glue from the back. He foolishly held the book over the glue kettle to steam the back, and the heat immediately caused the folds of the sections to shrink. Quite naturally, he was most distressed, but Hardy patiently repaired the damage by placing each section erect upon a grid above a pan of water and covering the whole to keep the moist air in among the leaves. Each day he stretched the moist sheet vertically at the fold until he removed all the waves and wrinkles and was able to press each pair of leaves between paper lined boards to restore their original flatness. On one of the fly leaves of the book there is a "Note du relieur," signed by Hardy, explaining that the large quantity of illustrations

29

made it necessary to create supplementary gatherings of these illustrations between the gatherings of the book proper. Otherwise he would have had to break the folds of the volume or construct a bad binding.

The most important showing of the Club Bindery's work was at the Grolier Club from 26 April through 12 May 1906. Except at the Dodd, Mead show of 1900 the Club Bindery had always exhibited in conjunction with other binders. Most of the 138 bindings displayed came from Hoe's collection. A catalogue with descriptions was written by Henry W. Kent, once librarian of the Grolier Club and later secretary of the Metropolitan Museum of Art, with an introduction by Beverly Chew.

Such elaborate treatment as that received by *The Scarlet Letter* on vellum can only be afforded for books of corresponding value, interest, and rarity, and many was the rare, valuable, and interesting title that came to the Club Bindery. Since Cornelia Hopkins' ledgers are lost, we must content ourselves with the descriptions of only a few of these volumes.

There were many incunabula and other early printed books. There were copies of that nobly illustrated folio printed by Anton Koberger, Hartmann Schedel's *Weltchronik*, 1493, both in the Latin and in the rarer German edition; Sweynheim and Pannartz' edition of Caesar's *Commentaries*, 1469; the fabulous Aldine *Hypnerotomachia Poliphili*, 1499; Pynson's edition of Sebastian Brant's *Shyp of Folys*, 1509; works from the presses of William Caxton, Wynkyn de Worde, and Thomas Berthelet; and one or possibly two copies of Burton's *Anatomy of Melancholy*, 1621. Holmes reports that when Hoe saw Marshall Lefferts' copy of Burton in the bindery, the former boasted with the pardonable pride of a collector that his copy was a half an inch taller. There were first folios of Chaucer and Spencer, and there was at least one group of the four Shakespeare folios. In addition, there were also a few of the vary rare Spencer and Shakespeare quartos.

One particularly amusing incident occurred in 1905 when Franklin's English edition of Cicero's *De Senectute* (Philadelphia, 1744), a volume described by Bruce Rogers as Franklin's "handsomest book," came in for binding. A few days earlier, a remark, ironical and humorous in intent, had been made by the

31

noted Canadian-British physician, surgeon, and bibliographer, William Osler, to the effect that men over sixty should be mercifully chloroformed, a scholium on the harsh treatment of the ageing person by business and industry around the turn of the century. This light remark was taken dead-pan by the metropolitan press and caused a flurry of mild public excitement, much to the embarrassment of the author. Osler had just been appointed Regius Professor of Medicine at Oxford; and, after leaving Baltimore where the embarrassing speech was made, he spent a few days in New York before sailing for England. This visit afforded the wags among Osler's medical friends an opportunity to add to the great man's embarrassment. They obtained Franklin's noble edition of Cicero's eulogy of the pleasures of old age to present to Osler as a classical rebuttal of his ironical advocacy of euthanasia. The little quarto was brought to the Club Bindery by Beverly Chew, who unfolded the plot to rib Osler before the entire staff and several patrons who were present, including Winston H. Hagen and Walter Gilliss. The book was bound in a handsomely tooled red crushed levant binding and was presented to Osler by his friends in the New York Medical Society at a dinner given in his honor on the eve of his departure for England. The much-sought-after Franklin rarity is now in the William Osler Library of McGill University in Montréal.

An unusual piece executed by the Club Bindery adorns a collection of vellum leaves signed by thousands of business men throughout America as a tribute to J. P. Morgan for his statesmanlike conduct in the financial panic in the summer of 1907. The vellum leaves of the testimonial were handsomely illuminated and were bound in dark blue crushed levant. The conventional design on the front and back covers consisted of a number of parallel lines in gold, broken midway by a design, the whole forming a panel. The doublure was also in blue levant and had parallel lines around the edges in gold and at the corners a special monogram, J.P.M., and the date 1907 in gold. Holmes assembled and forwarded the leaves; Hardy covered the book; and Paul Maillard finished it. The book is now in the Pierpont Morgan Library.

Shortly after the turn of the century many talented young American women began to turn to bookbinding. It is interesting to note that most of them hurried off to England to study under Cobden-Sanderson or to Paris to study under masters such as Domont, Badet, Provost, Noulhac, Cuzin, Maylander, and Mercier, and in Brussels under De Buhl and Jacobs. They did not realize that a proper approach to Hardy, the Maillards, and Holmes would have provided them with the best instruction in the world, at home in New York. Emily Preston, a student of Cobden-Sanderson and one of the best women bookbinders, wrote of the Club Bindery in *The Independent* for 8 December, 1910:

Here the highest class of French skilled labor produced works that were marvels of technical excellence. The workmen came out of the best Paris ateliers and all the equipment was imported, like the labor. The Club Bindery was short lived; a decade saw it come and go, and I think its failure lay in its limitations. The output went almost completely to collectors who owned the stock, the individual buyer having no part in its maintenance. But tho it is now entirely of the past, this bindery was of incalculable importance to American binders and their workmen, who saw the fine tooling those Frenchmen were capable of doing and learned many a salutary lesson of the value of technique.

It may readily be seen from Emily Preston's comment that the Club Bindery was exerting a powerful, even if indirect, influ-

33

ence on American binding; and she was one of the leaders of a small group of workers in the book arts who met in her New York shop on 14 November 1906 to organize the Guild of Book Workers. Forty-two persons joined to form a center for the collection and distribution of useful and reliable information in all fields of the book arts. Among those present was the late Frederic W. Goudy, and he printed the Guild's first yearbook at his Village Press.

Nevertheless, the Club Bindery did not have a direct influence on this group. None of the distinguished women bookbinders of the first part of this century, for example, Ellen Gates Starr, Elizabeth G. Marot, Edith Diehl, Alice Provost, and Marguerite Lahey, found their way to the Club Bindery for instruction. The Frenchmen were averse to imparting any knowledge of the art they had mastered only after long years of study and experience. They did not even like to be watched while at work. The only person who ever claimed to have studied at the Club Bindery is Curtis Walters, who distinguished himself as early as 1904 by developing an unusual mosaic technique in decorating his covers.

If Holden had been able to recruit a wide clientele for the Club Bindery, it might have had a longer history and a more direct influence. Instead, the trend was in precisely the opposite direction. Soon after the turn of the century Hoe acquired 106 shares of the bindery's stock, representing 51 per cent of the total. It is probable that he obtained control of the bindery and the burden of responsibility for it as a result of his insatiable desire to build an unrivalled private collection, and thanks to his ability to pay the high prices that had to be charged to keep the organization solvent. The bindery had always operated at a loss in the sense that it was necessary to charge several times what the individual jobs were worth commercially. The whole idea of the Club Bindery was epitomized in a remark by Hoe (quoted by Holmes) at a stockholders' meeting in 1908: "We have been interested in obtaining fine bindings, not profits!"

After 1902 the bindery did more and more work for Hoe, and as Holden's health failed, he looked to Hoe to assume leadership. Before Holden died on 8 June 1906 he asked Hoe to take full charge. Hoe immediately responded to Holden's request, and he fulfilled conscientiously his solemn obligation to furnish the craftsmen at the Club Bindery with the type of work which made the survival of the organization possible. Unfortunately, even Hoe did not have the resources to stand the continued strain of the expense of supplying enough work to keep the Club Bindery busy, and there was not enough demand from other collectors to support the business. It became evident that the bindery could not continue and would ultimately have to be closed, and Hoe began to take measures to close the bindery. At a private meeting of the officers in April, 1908, it was decided to dissolve the corporation. This decision was confirmed by the stockholders, and by the end of May they invested Beverly Chew and Walter Gilliss with power of attorney to handle the firm's affairs in the process of dissolution. Hoe was in Europe at the time. Written consent to the dissolution resolution, dated 10 June 1908, was not secured from all stockholders until the following January.

In the meanwhile, the work of the bindery continued as the officers were trying to work out some plan whereby the employees could purchase the stock. Among the generous proposals made to them was Hoe's offer to give them the use of the bindery plant free for a year until they could accumulate enough to buy the stock, but the craftsmen could not reach an agreement. None of them had ever learned to solicit business, and they had always depended on a patron whose business it was to place the work before them. Moreover, they never learned how to cope with native American competition, however inferior to their own work. Although the reputation of the Club Bindery could probably have carried it on for several years, the Frenchmen would never have been able to make the necessary adjustments, especially the adoption of less expensive production methods. They could survive only with the patronage of wealthy collectors who could pay high prices for their work. Otherwise the bindery would simply fold as soon as the new capital was exhausted.

Holmes' practical Anglo-Saxon approach to the problem, to earn the capital after a year's use of the shop without charge and then to adapt to American business methods, was over-ridden by the Frenchmen. He was a junior staff member and a national minority. The Frenchmen insisted that subscription by a number of patrons through Hoe was the only solution. Hoe told Hardy firmly that, while Chew and Hagen were prepared immediately to lend a hundred dollars towards a necessary two thousand dollar capital, the staff would have to secure the rest of the money. Moreover, Hoe was unwilling to sanction any plan that would not include Cornelia Hopkins, the only member of the staff who had a sense for management. The Frenchmen thought she was an unnecessary luxury.

Hoe's attitude toward the staff was paternal, but unmistakably friendly. In spite of a certain crispness of manner and a shell of official severity which great managers are supposed to have, Hoe revealed chinks in his iron exterior and a real warmth of his inner heart. He regarded the bindery staff with something akin to fondness. The bindery was his hobby, and his spirits were high whenever he was in the shop. He cherished Léon Maillard's work and often humored the great finisher. He gave a smile and often a pleasant word to all to whom he had reason to speak.

The employees accepted this protective relationship as being in the natural order of things. Life flowed pleasantly. The Frenchmen spoke of Hoe affectionately as "le grandpère." Holmes reports that long before dissolution was formally considered, Hoe had promised Hardy, Léon Maillard, and Cornelia Hopkins that he would give the bindery to the staff when the bindings needed for his library had been executed. Such was the general understanding in the shop, but the improvident craftsmen never thought of necessary preparations to put the business in shape for this contemplated change of ownership.

Once the dissolution resolution was proposed by the stockholders, Hoe, as the owner of fifty-one per cent of the stock, undertook at his own cost and risk to take steps to transfer the bindery to the staff by gift, partial gift, or sale. He purchased the remainder of the outstanding stock, probably at par, when the bindery was put up for auction at a sale held in the shop itself. The two most prominent New York binders of the day, Henry Stikeman and James Macdonald, were present, but they complied with a whispered request to offer no bid. Hoe bought the bindery at his own price, and Holmes states that it is his opinion that the price was equivalent to the full value of the stock as originally purchased. At least all the stockholders seemed to have been satisfied. Only one philistine was so bold as to complain that the stock had never paid dividends!

It is true that the panic of 1907 had dried up some potential sources of patronage for the binder, for example, Henry W.

Poor. On the other hand, the J. P. Morgan group survived the summer of 1907 in handsome style. Since Junius S. Morgan owned a share of Club Bindery stock at one time, and since the Pierpont Morgan Library was rich in manuscripts and early printed books, precisely the material that the Club Bindery needed, the Morgan Library could or might have gone far towards employing or partially employing the bindery staff indefinitely.

Long before the Club Bindery reached its final crisis, Cornelia Hopkins invited the late Belle da Costa Greene, the talented and bibliologically perspicacious Morgan librarian, to visit the bindery. That distinguished lady paid one visit and gave one small order for some half dozen three-quarter bindings, but nothing further was ever heard from her. Apparently there was a feeling of umbrage that had existed for a long time between Robert Hoe and J. Pierpont Morgan themselves; and, of course, no member of the Club Bindery staff would ever have had even the most remote opportunity to overcome this obstacle to Morgan patronage. Both men were such passionate collectors that one might well suspect that the barrier between them was one of rivalry for exclusiveness in a field which Thorstein Veblen would have classified as one of "conspicuous expenditure." The Morgan collection is particularly distinguished for its priceless manuscripts and comparatively few but superlative incunabula. The Hoe collection was matchless in its bindings and printed books. Had there existed a cordial friendship between these two giants of American bibliophilism, the destiny of the Club Bindery might have been materially affected.

For an entire year during which the dissolution and sale of the Club Bindery was in process, the staff was on a half-time schedule, the worst possible preparation for assumption of financial responsibility and ownership. If the members of the staff had any savings, their resources were consumed by daily expenses. No one suggested that the workmen should go out and dig up orders for themselves until it was too late. Hardy and the finishers objected with complete naïveté to carrying "the expense of the bookkeeper," Cornelia Hopkins. Léon Maillard used his great prestige within the staff to impose his ideas on the others. Immersed as he was in the minute problems of tooling and decoration, the larger issues of finance spelled out no definite meaning for him. The boresome problems of finance belonged on the polished desk of "le grand-père," not in the cloistered exclusiveness of the head finisher's room.

Little effort was made to reconcile the problems of the bindery with the stern directive of Hoe to Hardy that the staff must raise two thousand dollars capital. To be sure, Hardy and Holmes, both untrained and artless in the ways of business, made some effort to carry out Hoe's directive. They collected a few promises of capital from members of the Grolier Club, among them Arthur H. Scribner and Frederic R. Halsey. They continued calling upon potential patrons until they encountered Ernest Dressel North, a bookseller. He introduced the two binders to a customer, Willis Vickery of Cleveland, and the Ohioan began then and there to formulate plans to establish a fine bindery to be patronized by Cleveland's flourishing Rowfant Club.

When Hardy and Holmes reported to Léon Maillard (the dominant figure in the bindery in spite of the fact that Hardy was foreman), interest was diverted from the plan to raise working capital in New York, and attention was centered on the prospect in Cleveland. Only Holmes doubted that a provincial city could support a group of binding artists for whom even New York had been unable to provide sufficient patronage. Unfortunately, our forwarder and edge gilder was backward, bashful, and slow of speech, and he himself has said that he never had the kind of aggressiveness that this situation demanded.

There were days of feeble indecision during the last month of the life of the Club Bindery. There was some activity, but Hardy and Holmes made no further solicitations of working capital. The former was unwilling to allow the latter to go out alone, and Hardy was effectively restrained by Léon Maillard. Then Léon Maillard cut off all further discussion by announcing his final decision to go to Cleveland. Weary of months of bewilderment but still visibly doubtful, Hardy yielded to this decision. At least it was a decision. Other members of the staff were making their own plans. Paul Maillard, unmarried and longing for the boulevards of Paris, planned to return to his native land. Adolph Dehertog and his wife were quietly formulating arrangements to open a road house in Jersey. Hoe's magnificent gift was thrown away.

Holmes has recalled a dramatic moment at the end. He walked into the bindery as Cornelia Hopkins was telling Robert Hoe of Léon Maillard's fateful decision. Hoe, righteously indignant, turned upon the mild Englishman and accused him of being the author of the plan to move to Cleveland. He expressed the full measure of his indignation at Léon Maillard, whom he had befriended and whose temperamental outbursts he had tolerated so often. Bitterly and resentfully, he almost shouted at Holmes, "I shall close the bindery, pack it up, and put it in storage!"

After the bindery was closed, and in response to a request from Vickery, the tools were offered to the Rowfant Bindery, but the Rowfant officers felt that Hoe's price was prohibitive. He offered the entire plant for ten thousand dollars, a figure that was generous enough in view of the fact that the tools alone had cost far more. There was also an abundant stock of levant skins and all other material needed by the bindery.

The Club Bindery was closed in April, 1909. The last book

bound was *A Sketch of Cyrus K. Curtis* (of the Curtis Publishing Company), a fine example of the best work of the Gilliss Press. The tools and equipment were placed in temporary storage pending final settlement, but Hoe died in London on 22 September 1909 before final disposition could be made. It was not until almost two years later that a search for a buyer was made again. It seemed unlikely that any one binder in this country would have use for such an elaborate array of finishing tools, and therefore offers were solicited from binders here and abroad, but to no avail. Many of the tools and some of the equipment remain in use in the Macdonald bindery in New York today, for it was James Macdonald, who was gentleman enough not to bid at the auction, who finally purchased the largest part of the tools. From time to time, however, the tools appear in the hands of other binders, an old story of the continuity of binding traditions that is common in the history of the craft from late mediaeval times on.

Cleveland is perhaps second only to Chicago as a center of bookish culture in the Middle West. The Rowfant Club and the Western Reserve Historical Society, the fine traditions of humanistic scholarship at Western Reserve University and Oberlin College, and the cultural heritage from Connecticut have won much respect for books in Cleveland. But respect for books alone could not provide the support that a team of Hardy, Léon Maillard, and Holmes needed for business survival. That could be found only in Vienna, London, and Paris, not even in New York. It is not surprising that the Rowfant Bindery closed in 1913, four years after it opened.

Soon after Holmes and the two Frenchmen moved to Cleveland, they were joined by Hardy's brother-in-law, Gaston Pilon, who had been with Chambolle-Duru in Paris. The four men produced a goodly number of handsome bindings, comparable in every way to what the Club Bindery had achieved in New York, but the needed volume of orders was not forthcoming.

finisher, Léon Maillard, once the proud occupant of a bench in the atelier of Marius Michel, was even reduced to selling electric carpet sweepers all over Cuyahoga County. Vickery has told the story in a mixture of pride and disappointment in his essay on *The Rowfant Bindery*, privately printed in Cleveland in 1928.

Toward the end of World War I, Frank N. Doubleday of the Country Life Press in Garden City, Long Island, realized the public relations value of having a fine bindery in his establishment, and he brought Hardy, Léon Maillard, and Pilon back east. The unhappy, never fully stable Maillard, took his own life in 1921. Hardy and Pilon did many distinguished bindings; and while Hardy passed away first, Pilon continued to be active until the summer of 1951. The work of "the French binders" in Garden City was the last chapter in the history of the personnel of the Club Bindery. Many Pilon-Hardy bindings are in American private collections and libraries; they contribute heavily toward the preference of many American bibliophiles for French binding styles from the period around the turn of the century.

Holmes has said that the Club Bindery fell short of the traditional American ideal of triumph

43

Holmes was the first to leave, and he turned to a career of bibliographical scholarship that won him far greater distinction than any that he might have earned as a binder. The others did not fare so well. The master over apparently unsurmountable obstacles. Indeed, the obstacles to the continuing successful operation of a bindery catering to a few very wealthy collectors are unsurmountable in the United States of the twentieth century. Nevertheless, we must judge the Club Bindery, just as all other human institutions, by its works. Today a fine book with a Club Bindery imprint on the doublure will still fetch a premium at any auction, and its new owner, whether an individual or a library, will spread the gospel of art in binding in precisely the terms that would have been used by Hardy or Léon Maillard. English binding styles were brought to America by Matthews, the Launders, Macdonald, and the pupils of Cobden-Sanderson; German traditions propagated by Peter Franck, Gerhard Gerlach, Jean Eschmann, and the devotees of the Wiemeler school in the twenties and thirties have also had a powerful influence. Still, the forwarding techniques of Hardy and the incomparable decorative work of Léon Maillard have a perceptible and continuing influence on the practices of hand binders and the tastes of American collectors of the fifties. Above all, the standard of the finished product set by the masters of the Club Bindery is recognized by all connoisseurs of the art, regardless of their prejudices for one style or another.

From the library of W. Hugh Peal, New York

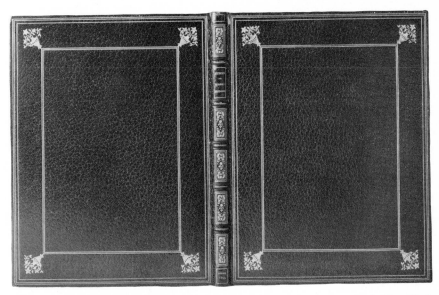

From the library of W. Hugh Peal, New York

From Princeton University Library
(Rubaiyat of Omar Khayyam)

Rare Books Division, Library of Congress
(John Gay's Fables)

Spencer Collection, New York Public Library
(Hawthorne's Scarlet Letter)

Pierpont Morgan Library, New York
(Testimonial to J. P. Morgan)

William L. Clements Library, University of Michigan
(John Smith's The True Travels of Capt. John Smith)

The University of Illinois Library
(Microcosmos)